Keepsake Crafts

FOR GRANDPA AND ME

BY MEGAN HEWES BUTLER

ILLUSTRATIONS BY FRANCESCA DE LUCA

ODD DOT 🦉 NEW YORK

Table of Contents

CHOOSE A CRAFT AND SPEND TIME TOGETHER!

Introduction

Dear Grandpa and Grandkiddo,

Welcome! I'm so glad you're both here. In your hands you hold a guide to minutes, hours, and days you can spend sharing memories—and creating new ones—across generations. Make crafts together that help you dream, connect, play, create, share, and remember. When you're finished, cherish these keepsakes or give them as gifts to spread the love.

Inside these pages, you'll find:

TIME TOGETHER ICONS

Use these time icons to help you select a project that fits your time together. Feel free to work at your own pace—these are just estimations to help you plan.

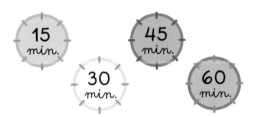

MOMENTS TO TREASURE

Use this heart icon to cue you in to places where you can stay in the moment together—whether taking a nature walk side by side, drawing your dreams, or collaboratively making up stories—these are the moments to simply enjoy being together.

SPECIAL MATERIALS

Use this star icon to know which projects use special materials (printed cardstock or stickers) from the back of the book.

Use the features above to help choose your first project. When you finish a craft, don't forget to sign and date the other side. Then share smiles creating two wonderful things together—a keepsake craft and a special memory!

Yours,

Megan Hewes Butler

You're a Star Art

Create stars in your eyes with this wall-worthy memento.

30 min.

PLUS A FEW HOURS TO DRY

GATHER THESE ITEMS:

- Newspaper or other scrap paper
- Paintbrush
- Large plate or tray
- 2 sheets of white or light-colored paper (11" x 17" [28 cm x 43 cm] or larger)
- Pencil or pen
- 2 pairs of scissors—1 for you and 1 for your grandkiddo
- Glue
- Washable paint (finger paint or tempera) in various colors

LET'S GET STARTED:

1. Cover your workspace and lay a sheet of large newspaper or scrap paper on top.

2. Roll up your and your grandkiddo's sleeves.

3. Place dollops of various colors of paint around the outside of your plate. Use the paintbrush to mix your first color in the middle of the plate.

4. Have your grandkiddo place one hand down in the paint until it covers their entire hand. Then press their hand firmly on the paper.

5. Next, it's your turn! Cover your own hand in paint, then stamp it on the paper.

6. Take turns stamping your hands back and forth until they stack, layer, and fill the paper. (Tip: Use the paintbrush to mix another color in the middle of the plate.)

7. Let the art dry for a few hours.

8. Flip over the paper and draw a large star. (Tip: If you don't get it the way you like on the first try, no worries! This will be the back, so you can try again.)

9. Cut out around the lines of the star.

10. Glue the back of your star to your remaining sheet of paper.

11. Take turns signing your names near one of your handprints. Over time, check your grandkiddo's handprint next to the artwork to see how they've grown!

ELLINGTON

GRANDPA

Toy Parachutes

Take a leap together with these classic flying toys.

TIME TOGETHER: **45 min.**

GATHER THESE ITEMS:

- 1-gallon plastic bag
- 2 photographs or drawn pictures— 1 of you and 1 of your grandkiddo
- Yarn or string
- 2 pairs of scissors—1 for you and 1 for your grandkiddo
- Tape
- 2 quarters

LET'S GET STARTED:

1. Cut off the top of your plastic bag, then cut around the seams until you have 2 square pieces of plastic.

2. Cut 1 piece of yarn about as long as your grandkiddo's arm. Then cut 3 additional pieces the same length to make 4 equal pieces of yarn.

3. Tape a piece of yarn to each corner of a plastic square.

4. Cut out the picture of your grandkiddo.

5. Tape a quarter in the middle of the back of the picture.

6. Tape the 4 loose ends of the string to the back of the picture (on top of the quarter), making sure that the strings are all even.

7. Have your grandkiddo repeat steps 2 through 6 to make a second parachute with *your* picture.

8. Take your parachutes to a high place and let them fly!

You Rock Photo Frame

Rock out together to make this unique frame to store your memories.

TIME TOGETHER: **45 min.** **PLUS A FEW DAYS TO DRY**

GATHER THESE ITEMS:

- Air-dry clay ◄------
- A small round saucer or plate
- A round-top drinking glass
- Toothpick
- Clear spray sealer (Grandpas only!)
- Various small rocks (see step 1)
- Photograph or small piece of art
- Optional: assortment of small craft items like beads, gems, or pom-poms

For another craft with air-dry clay, check out Superpowered Animal Pencil Holders

LET'S GET STARTED:

1. Go on a nature walk together and collect some small rocks of different colors and shapes—or find craft items like beads, gems, or pom-poms.

2. Take out a softball-sized piece of air-dry clay and divide the clay in half, 1 piece for you and 1 piece for your grandkiddo.

3. Together, knead each piece of clay.

4. Press and roll each piece of clay into a flat disc about ½" (1¼ cm) thick. Use your palms to smooth out the surfaces. (Tip: Add a little bit of water to your fingertips to perfect any cracks or sticky areas.)

5. Turn your saucer upside down and place it on top of 1 disc of clay. Press the toothpick through the clay all around the edges of the saucer. Remove the saucer and repeat on the other disc of clay.

6. Place down the glass in the center of one disc of clay. Use the toothpick to press through the clay all around the glass. Repeat on the other disc of clay.

7. Peel up the outer scraps and inner circles of clay so that 2 doughnut shapes remain—these will become your picture  frames. Press around the edges of the doughnut shapes with your fingers to smooth out any rough parts.

8. Press your rocks and other craft items into the clay frames to decorate them. Use a little bit of water to attach the items to the clay.

9. Leave the frames to dry using the instructions on the clay, usually about 3 days. Halfway through this drying time, flip over the frames.

10. **(Grandpas only!)** In a safe location, follow the instructions on the spray sealer and coat each frame, then let them dry.

11. Attach a picture or drawing to the back of each frame, facing up. Then display your memories around your homes.

Lovable Slime Monsters

Make lovable monsters—and memories—together with this easy slime recipe.

TIME TOGETHER: 30 min.

GATHER THESE ITEMS:

⭐ Cardstock from page 63
- 2 pairs of scissors—1 for you and 1 for your grandkiddo
- 4-oz. bottle of glue
- About 2 cups of foaming shaving cream
- 1 tablespoon of liquid laundry detergent
- Food coloring
- Medium-sized bowl
- Spoon
- Airtight container
- Optional: 1 teaspoon of hand or body lotion

LET'S GET STARTED:

1. Squeeze the whole bottle of glue into your bowl.

2. Decide together what color you'd like your lovable monsters to be. Add 5 to 7 drops of food coloring to the glue, then mix with your spoon.

3. Add the shaving cream to the mixture, then combine again with your spoon. (Tip: The shaving cream does not need an exact measurement.)

4. Add the liquid laundry detergent and mix one last time with your spoon.

5. Take the slime out of your bowl and knead it with your hands. It will be sticky at first, but keep going until it no longer sticks to your hands. If your slime remains sticky, add another tablespoon of detergent. If your slime is not stretchy enough, add 1 teaspoon of hand or body lotion.

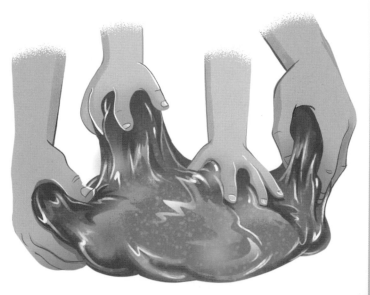

6. Cut out the monster pieces from your sheet of cardstock.

7. It's time to play! Take 2 handfuls of slime, 1 for each of you, and form the bodies of your monsters. Insert monster parts and accessories. How many monsters can you make? What stories can you tell?

8. To make your lovable monsters last forever, take a picture! Then store your slime in an airtight container for up to a week.

ROLL A DICE TO CHALLENGE EACH OTHER! DID YOU ROLL A 2? GREAT! ADD 2 FEET! HOW ABOUT A 6? ADD 6 EYES!

2 FEET?

1 TENTACLE?

3 EYES?

Custom Paper Gliders

Get a flying start on these paper gliders, and soon you'll be racing together.

TIME TOGETHER: **30 min.**

GATHER THESE ITEMS:

- ☆ Cardstock from page 65
- Drawing tools like crayons, colored pencils, or markers
- 2 paper straws
- 2 pairs of scissors—1 for you and 1 for your grandkiddo
- Tape
- 20 paper clips
- Optional: Small ball of clay

LET'S GET STARTED:

1. Cut out the wings and stabilizers from your cardstock—1 set for you, and 1 set for your grandkiddo.

2. Fold both of the stabilizers on the dotted lines so that they look like fins pointing up. Place a piece of tape across the bottom to hold the shape.

3. Lay out both gliders: Place a pair of wings near the front and a stabilizer at the back, right on top of each straw.

4. Use teamwork to secure the cardstock parts in place with pieces of tape underneath the straws.

5. Start with 5 paper clips to add a weighted nose to the front of each glider. Clip them to the straw, right in front of the wings.

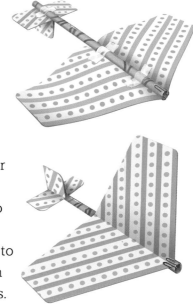

6. Give the gliders a test throw! (Tip: If your glider doesn't go very far, don't worry! Add up to 10 total paper clips to the nose, then add a small ball of clay for more weight.)

Aircraft Target Practice

This high-flying activity targets action games and silly memories together.

TIME TOGETHER: 15 min.

GATHER THESE ITEMS:

☆ Cardstock from page 67
● 1 large sheet of poster board (or several sheets of thick paper taped together)
● Drawing tools like crayons, colored pencils, or markers
● Round objects to trace like bowls, cups, or Frisbees
● 2 pairs of scissors—1 for you and 1 for your grandkiddo
● Paper gliders and airplanes ←--

Make your own with Custom Paper Gliders!

LET'S GET STARTED:

1. Lay out several round objects on your poster board, leaving enough space between each object for your flat palm to fit. (Tip: The objects should be larger than your aircrafts so they can fly through.)

2. Trace around each object.

3. Cut out the circles and decorate the poster with cut-outs from your cardstock sheet.. Assign points to each hole and write them on the poster. (Larger holes can be worth 1 point, and smaller holes can be worth 10 or more points.)

4. Hang up your poster, then stand side by side and aim at the holes with your paper gliders!

5. Create a more challenging version with these ideas:

★ Write one action next to each circle, like *twirl*. Whoever flies an aircraft through that target has to do the action!

★ On the backside of the poster, write one silly item next to each circle, like *rocket roller skates*. Whoever flies an aircraft through that target has to tell a quick imaginary story with that item!

Hanging Memories

Build a hanging balance sculpture to showcase your favorite memories.

TIME TOGETHER: **45 min.**

GATHER THESE ITEMS:

- 3 short sticks or chopsticks
- Hole punch
- String or yarn
- 2 pairs of scissors—1 for you and 1 for your grandkiddo
- Small memorable items (see step 1)

LET'S GET STARTED:

1. Go on a hunt inside and outside your home together. Collect small items that you like or that remind you both of your memories, such as:

   - Notecards you've sent or received
   - Small toys
   - Colorful bowties or neckties you've outgrown
   - Items from the workshop, like nuts, bolts, or wood scraps
   - Items from nature, like pine cones, rocks, or shells
   - Decorative items, like dried pasta shapes, pom-poms, buttons, or beads

2. Cut 8 pieces of string, each about as long as your grandkiddo's arm.

3. Cut 2 pieces of the arm's-length string in half.

4. Tie your longest piece of string around both ends of your longest stick. Hang it on a doorknob near your craft area.

5. Tie another piece of string around the middle of your second stick, then repeat with another piece of string and your last stick.

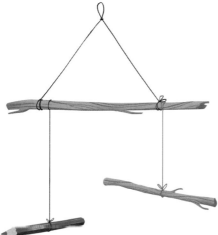

6. Tie each of the freestanding sticks onto an end of your hanging stick.

7. Work together to tie your collection of small items onto your remaining strings. You may be able to wrap around and knot some items, while others may need a hole punch. Add items at the ends or middles of the strings. (Tip: Adding several items in a row will add variety to your balance sculpture.)

8. Tie the strings of items onto the sticks. Add them to the longest stick or one of the shorter ones. Move each string right and left to balance out your sculpture. (Tip: If your sculpture is too heavy on one side, untie that string of items and move it to the other side.)

9. Hang your completed sculpture somewhere where you'll see it often. Which item is your favorite? Tell a story or a memory that you are reminded of!

Silly Surprise Pop-Up Card

Stick out your tongue with these silly pop-up cards!

TIME TOGETHER: 15 min.

GATHER THESE ITEMS:

- 4 sheets of colored paper
- 2 pairs of scissors—1 for you and 1 for your grandkiddo
- Drawing tools like crayons, colored pencils, or markers

LET'S GET STARTED:

1. Give 2 sheets of paper to yourself and 2 to your grandkiddo. Fold each sheet of paper in half, like a book, then open the sheets so they lay flat.

2. Draw a character on the right side of your papers—it can be any character with a large head and mouth. Talk together about your drawings!

3. Fold the paper back so that your character is folded in half, then cut a slit through the mouth.

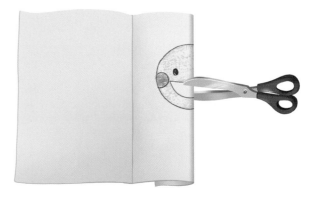

4. While the paper is still folded, cut a second slit a few inches below.

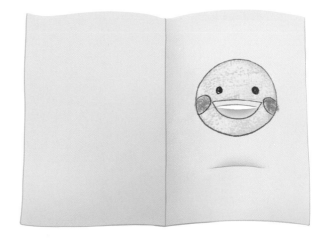

5. Cut a tongue strip from your other sheet of paper. It should be as tall as your card and almost as wide as your slits.

6. Weave the tongue strip through the slits.

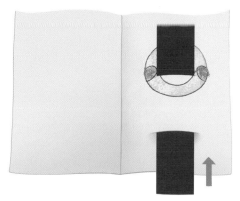

7. Fold over the top and crease it firmly. (Tip: Cut the end of your tongue into a shape if you'd like.)

8. Draw an arrow on the bottom of your strip. Pull down and push up on the strip to watch the tongue move and wiggle!

9. Write or draw messages inside your cards and give them to people you love.

MAKE MORE CARDS WITH DIFFERENT CHARACTERS OR ANIMALS—REAL OR IMAGINARY!

Any-Day Crackers

Big day? Rainy day? Make and break open these everyday crackers!

TIME TOGETHER:
TIME TOGETHER:

30 min.

GATHER THESE ITEMS:

⭐ Cardstock from page 69
- 2 or more toilet paper tubes (or a paper towel tube cut in half)
- 1 or more sheets of tissue paper
- 2 or more sheets of paper
- 2 pairs of scissors—1 for you and 1 for your grandkiddo
- Yarn or string
⭐ Optional: Drawings, photographs, or other paper artwork for cutting; drawing tools; "Use-anywhere stickers" from page 95

LET'S GET STARTED:

1. Work together to make and gather small fillings for your crackers: Write jokes, draw pictures, add a sweet treat, look for small nature treasures or jot love notes! Cut out and respond to the prompts from your cardstock sheet if you'd like.

2. Cut 4 pieces of yarn, each about the length of your hand.

3. Cut a sheet of tissue paper in half.

4. Lay each tube on its own sheet of tissue paper, centered at one end of the paper. Put your fillings inside and tightly roll the tissue paper around each tube.

5. Tie a piece of yarn around each end of excess tissue paper to secure the tubes closed.

6. Wrap a small piece of artwork around the outsides of your crackers, write a message, or add stickers.

7. Give the crackers to your loved ones to pop open!

Send-a-Hug Card

Pop this card in an envelope to share a hug with someone you love—even from far away!

TIME TOGETHER: 15 min.

GATHER THESE ITEMS:

- Close-up photograph or drawn portrait of your grandkiddo
- 2 sheets of construction paper
- 2 pairs of scissors—1 for you and 1 for your grandkiddo
- Glue
- Drawing tools like crayons, colored pencils, or markers

LET'S GET STARTED:

1. Cut out your grandkiddo's head from the photograph or drawn portrait.

2. Work together to trace around your grandkiddo's right and left hands on a sheet of paper. Then cut out the traced hands.

3. Fold the other sheet of paper in half the long way and cut along the crease to make 2 rectangles. (You'll use one and the other is extra.)

4. On a rectangle, glue your grandkiddo's head in the middle and hands on the ends.

5. Fold each arm in toward the face to form a hug that you can share!

6. Write a message inside to complete the card.

Patterned Spinners

Add some inertia to your day together with customized spinning top toys.

TIME TOGETHER: 45 min.

GATHER THESE ITEMS:

- 2 or more sheets of paper
- Roll of masking tape
- Drawing tools like crayons, colored pencils, or markers
- 2 pairs of scissors—1 for you and 1 for your grandkiddo
- Empty cereal box
- 2 quarters
- 8 pennies
- Glue

LET'S GET STARTED:

MAKE YOUR TOPS

1. Use the outside of your masking tape roll to trace and cut out 4 circles on each sheet of paper, making 8 circles in all.

2. Fold 2 of the circles in half twice to make 4 equal sections.

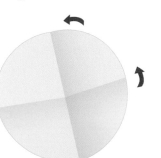

3. Open up the folded circles and poke a pencil through the center points.

4. One at a time, lay these circles on top of the other 6 circles as templates. Use your pencil to draw a dot in the exact center of each one.

5. Open the seams of your cereal box until it lays flat with the printed side facing up.

6. Glue the 2 folded circles onto the cardboard, then cut them out.

7. Make a small slit right on the center dot of each cardboard circle. (Tip: Pinch the cardboard in half right in the middle to make an easy cut.)

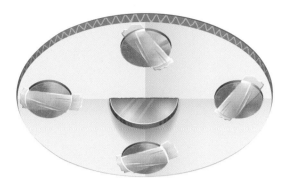

8. Press a quarter halfway through each slit on top of the cardboard circles. (Tip: If the quarter isn't held tightly in place, use a piece of masking tape on the top to secure it.)

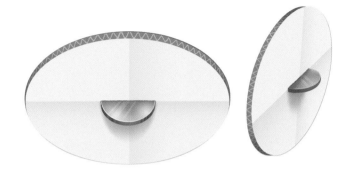

9. Tape 4 pennies evenly spaced around the outside edge of each top, with 1 penny on each fold.

10. Give your tops a spin! Can you get them both spinning at the same time? Which can spin for longer?

MAKE YOUR PATTERNS

1. Decorate your remaining paper circles with your drawing tools. Make different patterns like stripes or dots, or draw a picture of something you like to do together.

2. Make a small slit right on the center dot of each paper circle.

3. Press the decorated circles over the quarters on your tops.

4. Give them a spin to watch the colors swirl and change! Try again with a different patterned circle to see what happens.

You Are My Sunshine Painting

Make beaming sun rays together to brighten up your day.

TIME TOGETHER: 30 min.

GATHER THESE ITEMS:

☆ Cardstock from page 71
- 2 pairs of scissors—1 for you and 1 for your grandkiddo
- Washable paint (finger paint or tempera) in various colors
- Paintbrush
- 3 paper plates
- Large sheet of poster paper (at least 18" x 24", or 45¾ cm x 61 cm, any color)
- Optional: Aprons

LET'S GET STARTED:

1. Cut out the sun from your sheet of cardstock.

2. Roll up your and your grandkiddo's sleeves. (Or wear aprons for this painting project.)

3. In the center of one plate, place a large dollop of red paint. In the center of another plate, place a large dollop of yellow paint. In the center of your third plate, add a half dollop each of red and yellow paint. Help your grandkiddo mix the colors with a paintbrush to create orange.

4. Coat the back of the sun with orange paint. Use the paint to stick the sun to the center of your poster paper.

5. Help your grandkiddo to firmly press one hand down in the paint on a plate. Slowly move their palm around until it is covered in paint.

6. Press their hand down on the poster paper to create a handprint, making sure their fingers point away from the sun.

7. Practice a few more times together until your grandkiddo is ready to try on their own.

8. Talk about your favorite colors, and add them to the sunshine painting. Continue mixing colors on the plates (and on your hands!) to create varied colors and swirls in your finished rays of sunlight.

9. Add a few of your own handprints, too!

ONCE DISPLAYED, SEE HOW YOUR GRANDKIDDO'S HANDS GROW OVER TIME!

Secret Message Cipher

It's no secret—sending messages in code is sneaky (and enjoyable!).

TIME TOGETHER: 30 min.

GATHER THESE ITEMS:

⭐ Cardstock from page 73
- 2 pairs of scissors—1 for you and 1 for your grandkiddo
- 1 brad (or 1 small screw with nut)
- Paper
- Pencil

LET'S GET STARTED:

1. Cut out the 2 wheels from your cardstock sheet.

2. Stack the small wheel on top of the large wheel and press the brad or screw through the center star. Open up the brad on the back (or add the nut loosely onto the screw) to secure the circles together.

3. Turn the wheels so that both letter *A*s are lined up. Then turn the small wheel 3 letters to the right, so that the *A* in the small wheel is lined up with the *D* in the large wheel.

4. Now it's time to code: To start your message with the word *HI*, first look at the *H* in the small wheel. It is lined up with the letter *K*. Write down *K*. Repeat with the letter *I* (so you'll write down *L*). With the cipher set 3 letters to the right, *HI* is coded as *KL*.

5. Take turns writing coded messages, then trade them to read the secrets! (You'll have to take turns with the cipher, too—it's the only way to decode the messages.)

6. For your next set of coded messages, turn the small wheel a different number of letters—say 5 or 13 letters to the right.

7. Keep writing and sharing secret messages!

MAKE ANOTHER CIPHER TO SEND CODED MESSAGES OVER EMAIL OR THROUGH THE MAIL WHEN YOU ARE FAR APART!

Colorful Paper Flowers

Make flower power together with these rolled coffee filter beauties.

TIME TOGETHER: ⏱ **30 min.**

PLUS 30 MINUTES TO DRY

GATHER THESE ITEMS:

- Newspaper or other scrap paper
- 8 or more coffee filters
- Washable markers
- Spray bottle filled with water
- 2 or more pipe cleaners
- Markers
- Optional: Small vase or jar

LET'S GET STARTED:

1. Cover your workspace with newspaper or scrap paper.

2. Lay out your coffee filters in flat circles.

3. ♡ Decorate the coffee filters with washable markers.

4. Lightly spray the coffee filters with water until they are damp, then leave them to dry.

5. Stack 4 dry coffee filters together. Fold them in half, and then in half again.

6. Roll the stack of filters into a cone.

7. Wrap the end of one pipe cleaner tightly around the base of the cone about 4 times.

8. Use one hand to hold the pipe cleaner securely at the base. Use your other hand to gently pull and push the flower's petals apart. (Tip: This is even easier with teamwork!)

9. Have your grandkiddo repeat steps 5 through 8 to make a second flower—then keep going to make a full bouquet.

10. Display your flowers in a vase or jar, or give them to someone you love!

Wooden Memory Frames

Make a frame to showcase a photograph of the ones you love together.

TIME TOGETHER: **45 min.** PLUS OVER-NIGHT TO DRY

GATHER THESE ITEMS:

- 19 craft sticks
- Glue
- Photograph or drawing of you and your grandkiddo together
- Scissors
- Ribbon
- ☆ Optional: markers, glitter, or "Use-anywhere stickers" from page 95

LET'S GET STARTED:

1. Line up 11 craft sticks horizontally in rows.

2. Glue a craft stick vertically down each side of your stacked craft sticks. Then let them dry completely.

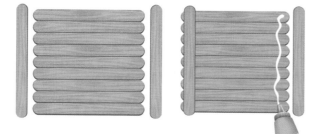

3. Cut your photograph to fit in the middle of the craft-stick frame—estimate or measure around 3" x 3" (7½ cm x 7½ cm).

4. Glue down your photograph or drawing face-up in the middle of your craft stick frame.

5. Glue an extra craft stick on each side to hide the edges of the photograph.

6. Use dots of glue to add 2 more craft sticks on the top and 2 more on the bottom to finish the frame, then let them dry overnight.

7. Decorate your frame with markers, glitter, or stickers. Talk about the memory in the frame and decide together which colors, patterns, and pictures to use around the outside.

8. Glue a loop of ribbon to the back to hang it. (Tip: These frames work great on doorknobs, bulletin boards, rearview mirrors—and as holiday ornaments and gifts!)

My Favorite Paperweight

Leave no stone unturned with these dazzling paperweights.

TIME TOGETHER: **30 min.**

PLUS OVER-NIGHT TO DRY

GATHER THESE ITEMS:

- 2 or more smooth stones, about the size of your palm
- Tissue paper
- 2 pairs of scissors—1 for you and 1 for your grandkiddo
- Mod Podge
- 2 paintbrushes
- Newspaper or other scrap paper
- ⭐ "Use-anywhere stickers" from page 95

LET'S GET STARTED:

1. Choose 1 stone for each of you, then wash and dry them completely.

2. Cover your workspace with newspaper or scrap paper.

3. Cut strips and shapes from your tissue paper.

4. Plan out your designs by talking together about your favorite colors, patterns, and pictures.

5. Lay small pieces of tissue paper on top of each of your stones. Apply thin layers of Mod Podge on top of the tissue paper while pressing the shapes down onto the stones.

6. Have your grandkiddo repeat step 5 with more pieces of paper. Cover both stones completely, or leave some parts exposed. Layer the tissue paper to make fun colors and shapes, or create patterns or pictures of your favorite things! (Tip: Add stickers too, but make sure to also cover them with Mod Podge!)

7. Let your paperweights dry overnight. (Tip: If they are still tacky in the morning, let them dry for another day.)

8. Use the paperweights where you'll see them and remember each other! They work great as decor on a desk, to hold down your artwork, or displayed in a bowl.

Yarn Art Cards

String together new memories—and make cards perfect
for giving to those you love!

YOU ARE A STAR!

TIME TOGETHER: 30 min.

GATHER THESE ITEMS:

- ☆ Cardstock from pages 75 & 77
- • 2 pairs of scissors—1 for you and
  1 for your grandkiddo
- • Thumbtack
- • Yarn
- • 2 large needles or plastic embroidery
  needles
- • Glue
- • 2 sheets of colorful cardstock or paper
- • Drawing tools like crayons, colored
  pencils, or markers

LET'S GET STARTED:

1. Cut out the templates from your cardstock
   sheet.

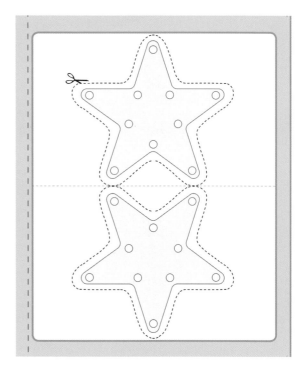

2. Punch your thumbtack through all of the
   holes on the templates. (Tip: These small
   holes will make it easier for the large
   needles to push through in steps 5 and 6.)

3. Cut 2 pieces of yarn, each a little longer
   than your grandkiddo's arm.

4. Tie a knot in one end of each piece of yarn. Thread the free ends of each piece through a needle.

5. Work side by side with your own templates and needles: Start by threading through any hole on the back of your templates to ensure that the knots stay on the backs.

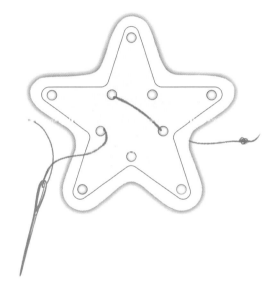

6. Continue threading through holes in any order you like. The order you pick will make your own unique designs! (Tip: Try going through each hole more than once.)

7. When your design is done, or when your yarn runs out, push your needle through to the back of the card and knot that end of the yarn.

8. Fold a piece of your cardstock or paper in half. Glue the template to the front to make your card.

9. Write messages to each other or to your loved ones, or decorate your cards however you'd like.

CREATE MORE YARN ART WITH YOUR OWN BLANK PAPER! SIMPLY DRAW A DESIGN WITH DOTS AND START AT STEP 2!

Winter Season Handprint Tree

Put your hands together to make these keepsake seasonal tree decorations.

TIME TOGETHER: 45 min.

GATHER THESE ITEMS:

- 6 or more sheets of drawings, paintings, or other 2-D artwork for cutting
- Construction paper
- 2 pairs of scissors—1 for you and 1 for your grandkiddo
- Pencil
- Glue
- Tape
- ☆ Optional: glitter, cotton balls, pom-poms, or "Use-anywhere stickers" from page 95

LET'S GET STARTED:

1. Have your grandkiddo place their hand, with fingers open, near the edge of one piece of artwork.

2. Trace around your grandkiddo's hand.

3. Place the hand in another location on the same piece of art—you may be able to trace 2, or even 3 or 4, handprints per page without overlapping them. Help your grandkiddo trace a few of your handprints, too! Keep tracing on more sheets until you have about 12 hands in all.

4. Work together to cut out all the handprints.

5. Roll a sheet of construction paper into a tall cone shape and secure it with tape.

6. Trim the bottom off the cone so that it sits flat.

7. Glue the back of the palm from a cut-out handprint to the bottom of the tree. Repeat this step to add each hand around the cone and up the tree.

8. Wrap the last hand around the top of the cone to create the final shape.

9. Decorate your trees with stickers, glitter, or even "snowy" cotton balls!

FOR LARGER TREES, ROLL YOUR CONE FROM A LARGER SHEET OF PAPER.

Cereal Catapult Game

Make an easy DIY catapult to fling cereal—and earn points for visiting your favorite places!

TIME TOGETHER: 45 min.

GATHER THESE ITEMS:

- Craft stick
- Bamboo (or plastic) spoon
- 2 rubber bands
- Pencil
- A large piece of cardboard
- 2 pairs of scissors—1 for you and 1 for your grandkiddo
- Glue
- A handful of large pieces of cereal (or pom-poms)
- Markers
- ⭐ Optional: paper bowls, plates, or cups; construction paper; pipe cleaners; or "Use-anywhere stickers" from page 95

LET'S GET STARTED:

1. To make your catapult, stack your spoon on top of your craft stick and secure the bottoms together with a rubber band.

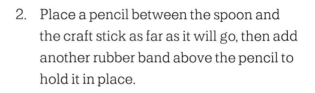

2. Place a pencil between the spoon and the craft stick as far as it will go, then add another rubber band above the pencil to hold it in place.

3. Test your catapult by placing a piece of cereal on the spoon. Pull the top of the spoon down and let it fly! (Tip: Adjust how the catapult flings by moving the pencil closer to, or farther away from, the bottom of the spoon.)

4. Cut open your cardboard into one long, flat piece and place your catapult at one end.

5. Create 5 targets with your paper bowls, plates, cups, construction paper, or pipe cleaners. The targets can be large or small, and have tall sides, short sides, or no sides.

6. Talk about your 5 favorite places to go together. Write the name of one place on each target. Assign 50 points to one favorite place, then 40 points, 30, 20, and 10 to the others.

7. Take turns loading up the catapult and shooting 5 pieces of cereal each. Which places did you get to visit? Add up your points to see who won!

Tower of Memories

Build a classic card pyramid together—and top it off with your loved ones as kings and queens.

TIME TOGETHER: **30 min.**

GATHER THESE ITEMS:

- ☆ Cardstock from page 79
- 2 pairs of scissors—1 for you and 1 for your grandkiddo
- Glue
- Drawing tools like crayons, colored pencils, or markers
- An old deck of cards
- ☆ Optional: "Use-anywhere stickers" from page 95

LET'S GET STARTED:

1. Cut out the cards from your cardstock sheet.

2. Draw on the cards to record your memories and cast your family as royalty, or add stickers to create a special design.

3. Balance 2 cards to form a triangle. Then balance a second triangle next to the first.

4. Slowly lay 1 card on top, like a roof.

5. Build higher by balancing another triangle of cards on top of the roof card.

6. Build higher still by building wider: balance another triangle next to the base 2. Lay another card on top to extend the roof.

7. Repeat steps 4 through 6 until your tower is towering! Top it off with your handmade cards.

8. Have fun collapsing your tower and building again with your custom cards. Can you build it taller? Wider? Which card will reign at the top?

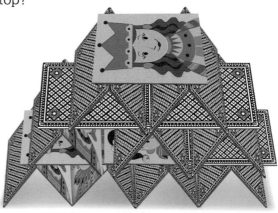

Give a Bird a Cookie

Create birdseed treats together to hang outside or give as gifts.

TIME TOGETHER: **15 min.**
PLUS OVER-NIGHT TO DRY

GATHER THESE ITEMS:

- 1 packet of unflavored gelatin
- 2 tablespoons of cold water
- ⅓ cup of boiling water
- Large bowl
- Spoon
- 2 cups of birdseed
- 4 or more favorite cookie cutters
- Nonstick cooking spray
- Baking pan
- Paper straw
- A piece of string for each cookie cutter (each about as tall as your grandkiddo)

LET'S GET STARTED:

1. Add your gelatin and 2 tablespoons of cold water to the bowl and let the mixture rest for 1 minute.

2. **(Grandpas only!)** Add your boiling water to the mixture. Gently stir for about 3 minutes until the gelatin is dissolved.

3. Add your birdseed and continue to stir until well combined.

4. Lay your cookie cutters out on the pan and coat them with nonstick spray.

5. Spoon the birdseed and gelatin mixture into each cookie cutter.

6. Press down on the mixture to pack it tightly in each mold.

7. Make a hole in the thickest part of each shape, usually the middle, with your straw.

8. Place the pan in the refrigerator overnight to set.

9. Carefully pop out the birdseed treats from the cookie cutters and thread a piece of string through each hole.

10. Tie a knot in each treat string to make them ready to give away or to hang outside for the birds! Watch together to see what birds visit for a treat.

Mapping Memories Puzzle

Put today on the map! Create a handmade puzzle to share memories and play together.

TIME TOGETHER: **30** min.

PLUS OVER-NIGHT TO DRY

GATHER THESE ITEMS:

- Newspaper or other scrap paper
- Pre-printed or hand-drawn map of somewhere you live, have memories of, or want to go together!
- Large sheet of chipboard (or an empty cereal box, opened up flat)
- Paintbrush
- Mod Podge or other craft glue
- 2 pairs of scissors—1 for you and 1 for your grandkiddo
- Optional: 2 to 3 hardcover books

LET'S GET STARTED:

1. Cover your workspace.

2. If you are using a cereal box, cut out one of the large, flat rectangles. Take care not to include any folds or seams. Lay the printed side up for the next step.

3. Lay your map on top of your chipboard or cereal box piece. If it is too large, talk together about which parts you want to keep, and cut the map to fit.

4. Coat the back of your map with Mod Podge. Place it sticky-side down on the chipboard or cereal box piece and press down until it's smooth. (Tip: For the best results, stack some hardcover books on top and let it dry for about an hour.)

5. Coat the front of your map with Mod Podge and let it dry overnight.

6. Cut your dried map into puzzle pieces in any shape and size—or cut it out along roads, paths, or rivers.

7. Assemble your puzzle together and talk about the places you see and where you'd like to go.

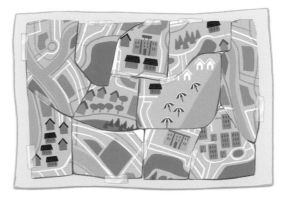

Nailed String Art

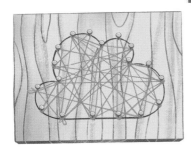

You've nailed it! Wrap up these colorful shapes to save and share.

GATHER THESE ITEMS:

- Wooden painting panel or wooden board of any size
- 20 to 30 small nails with heads (about ¾" or 2 cm long)
- Hammer
- Pencil
- String
- 2 pairs of scissors—1 for you and 1 for your grandkiddo

LET'S GET STARTED:

1. Talk together about shapes you see around you—perhaps a shell, bird, flower, cloud, car, dog, or something else. Choose 1 shape together and draw an outline of the simple shape on your board.

2. Draw about 20 to 30 evenly spaced dots around the outside of your shape. Each dot should be about ½" (1¼ cm) apart.

3. **(Grandpas only!)** Hammer a nail into each dot.

4. Cut a piece of string about twice as long as your grandkiddo's arm.

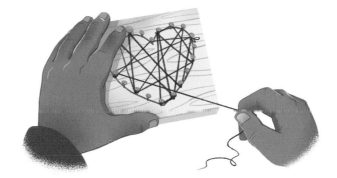

5. Tie one end of the string around one nail with a sturdy knot.

6. Take turns looping the thread around the other nails to create a design—go to each nail in order, or randomly. Wrap each nail once or multiple times to make a denser piece of art. (Tip: Tie on another color of string and keep wrapping!)

7. When you're satisfied with your design, tie the string to a nail and trim the end.

Superpowered Animal Pencil Holders

Tell stories together about your favorite animals (and their made-up superpowers!) while you sculpt these pencil holders.

TIME TOGETHER: **30** min. PLUS A FEW DAYS TO DRY

GATHER THESE ITEMS:

- Wax paper
- Air-dry clay
- 2 pencils
- Acrylic or tempera paint
- 2 paintbrushes
- Optional: fork or toothpick

For another craft with air-dry clay, check out You Rock Photo Frame

3. Talk together about your favorite animals and each pick one to make.

4. Form your balls of clay into the shapes of your favorite animals. Bend, pinch, and roll to create the legs, tails, wings, and ears that your animals have.

(Tip: Add a little bit of water to your fingertips to perfect any cracks or sticky areas or to attach 2 pieces of clay together.)

LET'S GET STARTED:

1. Cover your workspace with a sheet of wax paper.

2. Roll 2 egg-sized amounts of air-dry clay into balls, 1 for each of you.

5. Talk together: If you could each give your animals one superpower, what would it be? Add details to your animals for these special superpowers: Fins! A force field! Bouncy legs! A mouth for talking to you! A special eye to read your mind! (Tip: Use your fork or toothpick to carve into your clay to make fur, claws, or other small details.)

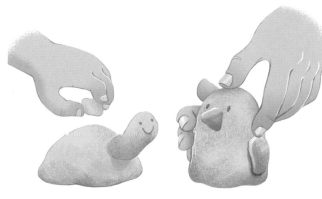

6. Press the pencils into the tops of your animals until they are almost all the way to the bottom, and then remove them.

7. Follow the instructions on the clay's package and allow your animals to dry, usually about 3 days.

8. When the animals are hardened, place them back on your wax paper and paint them. Let them dry for another day.

9. Place your pencils back into the holes you made in your animals and store them near your notebooks or desks.

USE THE LEFTOVER CLAY TO MAKE MORE ANIMALS TOGETHER. THEN MAKE UP A STORY TOGETHER ABOUT YOUR ANIMALS AND THEIR SUPERPOWERS!

Melted Abstract Artwork

Transform a collection of old crayons into collaborative works of art.

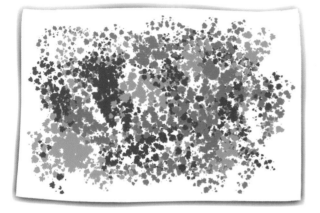

LET'S GET STARTED:

1. Peel off all the labels from your crayons and throw them away.

2. Create piles of wax shavings by twisting your crayons in the pencil sharpener.

TIME TOGETHER: **45 min.**

GATHER THESE ITEMS:

- Handful of old or broken crayons
- Handheld pencil sharpener
- Muffin tin
- 2 small baking pans (or 1 large one)
- 4 sheets of paper
- Iron and ironing board
- Parchment paper
- 2 dish towels
- 2 pairs of scissors—1 for you and 1 for your grandkiddo
- Optional: spoon

3. Collect the shavings in your muffin tin— mix the colors together, or keep each color separate.

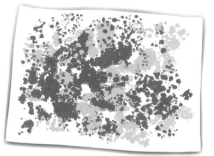

7. When the wax looks melted, carefully remove the paper and peel the parchment off the top. Your art is ready!

4. Place a sheet of paper in each baking pan. Use your fingers or a spoon to spread the crayon shavings over your paper to make a picture, a pattern or design, or just a spread of colors.

8. When you want to melt another sheet, recreate the "sandwich" from step 5.

9. Use your designs to make cards and artwork for those you love.

5. Set up your ironing station: Place a dish towel and then a sheet of parchment paper on your ironing board. Place your paper with crayon wax on next. Top it off with a second sheet of parchment paper and a second dish towel. (Your final "sandwich" should be: towel, parchment, paper with crayon wax, parchment, then towel.)

6. **(Grandpas only!)** With your iron on low, slowly melt the crayon shavings. Move the iron over the top in quick motions (lasting only a few seconds) and check to see if the wax is melted. (Tip: It usually only takes 10 to 15 seconds total to melt the wax.)

Growing in Thankfulness

Let your thankfulness "stick" out with this nature project for all seasons.

TIME TOGETHER: **45 min.** PLUS OVERNIGHT TO DRY

GATHER THESE ITEMS:

- ☆ Cardstock from page 81
- Newspaper or other scrap paper
- Acrylic or tempera paint
- 2 or more paintbrushes
- 2 pairs of scissors—1 for you and 1 for your grandkiddo
- 5 sheets of colorful paper
- Drawing tools like crayons, colored pencils, or markers
- Glue
- 2 sticks (see step 1)
- Optional: Several leaves (see step 4)

LET'S GET STARTED:

1. Go on a nature walk together and collect 2 sticks—1 for you and 1 for your grandkiddo. They can be the length of your arm, or as tall as your grandkiddo! Brush them off so they are clean.

2. Back inside, cover your workspace with newspaper or scrap paper.

3. Paint your sticks in full colors, or add stripes, dots, or other designs!

4. Let the sticks dry overnight. While you wait, cut out the leaf shapes from your cardstock sheet. (Tip: Trace leaves from outside or from the inside back cover of this book for a bigger collection!)

5. Cut out 5 or more leaf shapes for each stick.

6. Talk together about things you are each thankful for, and write or draw one thing on each leaf.

7. When the sticks are dry, glue your leaves to your sticks. Display on a table or shelf, or stand them up in a vase.

Always Find My Love Collage

Make collage art featuring your favorite memories—
then play search-and-find!

SLED
HAT
CLOUD
SHOE
DOG

TIME TOGETHER: **45 min.**

GATHER THESE ITEMS:

- Sheet of paper (at least 8½" x 11", or 21½ cm x 28 cm)
- Glue
- 2 pairs of scissors—1 for you and 1 for your grandkiddo
- Photographs, drawings, and magazines for cutting
- 2 or more index cards or other small pieces of paper
- 2 or more pencils
- ☆ Optional: "Use-anywhere stickers" from page 95

LET'S GET STARTED:

1. Talk about your favorite things, places, and memories. Look at your photographs, drawings, and magazines together and cut out pictures that remind you both of these favorites.

2. Glue the cutouts onto your paper. (Tip: Glue the largest pictures first and the smaller pictures last so that you can see them all in the finished collage.)

3. When the collage is finished, gather 2 index cards: 1 for you and 1 for your grandkiddo. Write or draw 5 things you each see in the collage.

4. Switch cards with each other, then search for the items listed on the card. Can you find them all?

Warm Fuzzies Bowl

Go around and around making warm, fuzzy memories—and you'll soon have bowls to store little treasures!

LET'S GET STARTED:

1. Cut out the bowl template from your cardstock sheet.

2. Lay the template on top of 1 paper plate and trace each of the 11 triangle slits, then repeat with the second plate.

TIME TOGETHER: 30 min.

GATHER THESE ITEMS:

- ★ Cardstock from page 83
- • 2 pairs of scissors—1 for you and 1 for your grandkiddo
- • 2 paper plates
- • Pencil
- • Yarn in multiple colors
- • Tape
- • Glue stick

3. Cut out the 11 triangle slits from each plate.

4. Each of you choose a color of yarn to begin each bowl. Tape the end of the strand to the middle of the underside of a plate.

5. Pull the yarn up through any triangle.

6. Take turns weaving the yarn up and down through each triangle slit, so that the yarn goes over and under alternating flaps of the paper plate. Pull the yarn to keep it tight as you go—this will cause the flaps to start to bend upward and form your bowl.

7. As you continue weaving around and around, talk about your favorite colors. Cut your current strand of yarn to change colors, then tie the cut end to the new yarn color and continue weaving.

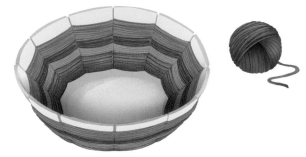

8. Stop weaving when you reach about a finger's width from the top of your bowl. Add glue around the remaining inside of the paper plate.

9. Continue wrapping and pressing yarn into the bowl, securing it to the glue. When you reach the top, cut the strand and tuck the end in to hide it.

10. Add glue to the bottom-middle of your bowl. Take a piece of yarn and wrap a circle around and around your bowl until you hit the center and can no longer see any of the paper plate left. Press down firmly to secure the yarn into the glue.

11. Use your bowls to store treasures and memories of your time together!

Leaf Portraits

Turn over a new leaf together while making portraits of those you love.

TIME TOGETHER: 30 min.

GATHER THESE ITEMS:

- A few sheets of paper
- Drawing tools like crayons, colored pencils, or markers
- Glue
- Various outdoor items (see step 1)

LET'S GET STARTED:

1. Go on a nature walk together and talk about what you see. Collect leaves, grass, twigs, bark, pine needles, pine cones, seeds, flowers, or other natural items in your area.

2. Back at home, sit side by side and talk about people you love. Choose one person you love and draw their portrait on a sheet of paper—ask your grandkiddo to do the same. Focus on their faces, making sure to draw eyes, a nose, a mouth, ears, and other details.

3. Play with your nature items on top of the face to form hair, earrings, a hat, a crown, a collar, or more.

4. Glue each nature item to your portrait.

5. Display your art for today, or take a picture to save it forever!

Collaborative Fruit and Veggie Stamping

Make fruit and veggie art with the apple of your eye.

TIME TOGETHER:

30 min.

PLUS A FEW HOURS TO DRY

GATHER THESE ITEMS:

- Newspaper or other scrap paper
- Blank notecards and envelopes
- Clean fruits and veggies for stamps
- Cutting board and knife
- Paint tray or small dish
- Acrylic or tempera paint

This activity works best with broccoli, okra, apples, peppers, celery, lemons, brussels sprouts, carrots, or corn on the cob!

LET'S GET STARTED:

1. Cover your workspace with newspaper or scrap paper.

2. **(Grandpas only!)** Cut your fruits and veggies into different pieces—cut some in half the long way and some the short way. See what shapes and textures you can make!

3. Squeeze a small dollop of paint into your paint tray.

4. Talk about your favorite fruits and veggies and choose one to start with. Press the cut side into the paint to cover the whole surface like a stamp and ink.

5. Have your grandkiddo stamp the fruit or veggie onto your paper.

6. Repeat steps 4 and 5 together with more fruits and veggies and more paint colors. See what designs or pictures you can make!

7. When your papers are dry, create cards and envelopes with them to share colorful messages with those you love.

Hanging Together Wall Art

Hang out together while you turn bright shapes, memories, and artwork into a wall hanging to hold on to.

TIME TOGETHER: 60 min.

GATHER THESE ITEMS:

- ★ Cardstock from page 85
- A stick, wooden dowel, or yardstick at least as long as your grandkiddo's arm
- 2 pairs of scissors—1 for you and 1 for your grandkiddo
- Glue
- String
- Drawings, paintings, or photographs for cutting (plain construction paper will also work)

LET'S GET STARTED:

1. Cut out the pieces from your cardstock sheet.

2. Cut other shapes from your drawings, paintings, photographs, or paper. You'll want a pile of around 100 or more shapes. While you cut and count, talk about memories and dreams for the various numbers as ages: What does your grandkiddo want to do at age 14? What do you remember? Where might your grandkiddo want to live when they are 40? Where did you live?

3. Cut 10 pieces of string, each longer than your grandkiddo's arm—with some as tall as your grandkiddo!

4. Start with 1 piece of string for each of you: Add glue to the back of 1 shape, place the string in the middle, and then make a sandwich with another shape on top. (Tip: It looks great when the shapes on both sides match. It also looks great when they *don't!*)

5. Add 5 or more sets of shapes to the string in a row. The shapes can be touching, spaced far apart, or located wherever you want along the string. Talk together about your favorite colors, patterns, or artwork that you are adding.

6. Tie one end of the string to your stick.

7. Repeat steps 4 through 6 until you are out of shapes or strings.

8. Arrange the strings across the top of the stick until they are spread out so you can see all your shapes.

9. Hang your wall art in a place where you will see your handiwork! Tie more strings over time to add more colorful memories.

A Bouquet to Share

Everything's coming up roses with this creative handful of flowers.

TIME TOGETHER: **15** min.

GATHER THESE ITEMS:

☆ Cardstock from page 87
● 6 or more sheets of colorful paper
● 2 pairs of scissors—1 for you and 1 for your grandkiddo
● Glue

LET'S GET STARTED:

1. Trace your hand and your grandkiddo's hand on a sheet of paper, then cut them out.

2. Cut 3 strips each from the short ends of different colored papers.

3. Cut out the shapes from your cardstock sheet.

4. Work side by side: Glue your hand and colorful strips on a blank sheet of paper—and have your grandkiddo do the same. (Tip: Glue the strips on first, under the hand, so that it looks like the hand is holding flower stems.)

 5. Play together by stacking, layering, and organizing the shapes into geometric flower designs.

6. Glue the backs of each flower onto their own stems.

7. Display your bouquets or give them away to people you love.

Artwork All Year Calendar

Turn pieces of art into a calendar you can use all year.

TIME TOGETHER: 45 min.

GATHER THESE ITEMS:

☆ Cardstock from page 89
- 2 pairs of scissors—1 for you and 1 for your grandkiddo
- Glue
- 12 handmade drawings or paintings
- Hole punch
- Chopstick or wooden skewer
- String

LET'S GET STARTED:

1. Cut out the month strips from your cardstock sheet.

2. Talk together about the artwork to see which fits best with each month. Then glue a calendar strip to each piece of art.

3. Put the art in order from January through December, and line up the tops to make a stack of 12 sheets.

4. Punch 3 holes across the top of the stack through all 12 sheets.

5. Cut 3 pieces of string, each about as long as your grandkiddo's hand.

6. Thread each string through a hole in the calendar. Wrap the strings around the chopstick and thread them back through their holes. Secure them tightly with knots on the back of the art.

7. Cut 1 piece of string as long as your grandkiddo's arm.

8. Tie an end of the string to each end of the chopstick.

9. Mark the calendar with special family days!

GRANDSON'S BIRTHDAY!

Craft Stick Family

Create one big happy family using simple craft sticks.

TIME TOGETHER: 30 min.

GATHER THESE ITEMS:

- Handful of large craft sticks
- Permanent markers in multiple colors
- Various craft items, like colorful tape, scraps of fabric or paper, yarn, buttons, and glue

2. Choose 1 person and 1 craft stick to start with for each of you, and begin by drawing a face at the top.

3. Add creative clothing next: Wrap tape or yarn around the stick for a shirt, or cut out fabric for pants or a skirt.

4. Draw on legs and feet.

5. Add other details like yarn for hair, buttons on the shirt, or even a hat!

6. Make more craft sticks for other people in your family or your friends.

7. When you are done, use the sticks to tell stories or act out memories together.

LET'S GET STARTED:

1. Talk together about people in your family—those who are nearby and those who may be far away.

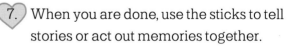

MAKE STICKS FOR YOUR PETS, TOO!

Twig Burst Wreath

Gather twigs together to build a keepsake wreath that works in all seasons.

TIME TOGETHER:

60 min.

PLUS OVERNIGHT TO DRY

GATHER THESE ITEMS:

- Round plate
- Piece of cardboard as large as your plate
- Pencil
- Scissors
- String
- Wood or craft glue
- Photographs of your family
- 30 or more twigs (see step 6)

LET'S GET STARTED:

1. Lay the plate on top of your piece of cardboard, then trace and cut around the outside.

2. Draw and cut out a smaller circle, about the size of your hand, in the middle of the circle you cut in step 1. (Tip: It does not need to be perfect because it will be hidden later.)

3. Cut a piece of string as long as your grandkiddo's arm.

4. Loop the string through the middle of the first circle and tie a knot so it hangs from the yarn.

5. Go on a nature walk together and collect 30 or more twigs that are about as tall as your cardboard circle. (Tip: Break longer twigs into pieces if needed. They do not need to be exact.)

6. Back inside, line up the ends of the twigs to the inside circle so they form a clean edge, but let the other ends of the twigs form a jagged shape outside the circle.

7. Pick up 1 stick at a time. Add a good amount of glue to one end of each stick, then place them back down.

8. Let the wreath dry overnight.

9. Decorate your wreath with photographs, then hang it on a door or mantel!

THIS WREATH IS GREAT FOR ADDING DECORATIONS FROM OTHER PROJECTS, LIKE COLORFUL PAPER FLOWERS!

Wild Expressions

These silly faces are definitely a laughing matter.

LET'S GET STARTED:

1. Cover your workspace with newspaper or scrap paper, then place 2 sheets of paper on top.

2. Roll up your and your grandkiddo's sleeves.

3. Place a few dollops of various colors of paint around the outside of your plate. Use your paintbrush to mix your first color in the middle of the plate.

4. Take turns placing one hand down in the paint until it covers your entire handprint. Then firmly stamp your hands in the center of a sheet of paper.

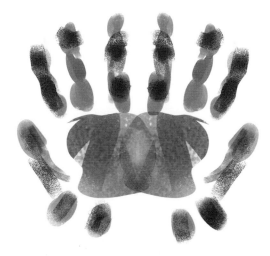

TIME TOGETHER: **45 min.** PLUS A FEW HOURS TO DRY

GATHER THESE ITEMS:

- Newspaper or other scrap paper
- Several sheets of paper (8.5" x 11" [21½ cm x 28 cm] or larger)
- Washable paint (finger paint or tempera) in various colors
- Paintbrush
- Large plate or tray
- Various craft supplies, like googly eyes, pom-poms, pipe cleaners, cotton balls, twist ties, paper straws, recycled bottle caps, or colored paper
- Glue
- Scissors

5. Repeat step 4 with your other hands. Stamp your hands right next to the first prints to make one large shape.

6. Repeat steps 4 and 5 on new sheets of paper until you have made a few sets of handprints each. Add variations—point your fingers out, squeeze them together, or even add 4 handprints in 1 large stack!

7. Let the paint dry for a few hours or overnight.

8. Play with and move the craft supplies around on top of the handprints to make silly faces. Turn the papers to look for new features, too! Can you create teeth? Or tentacles? Or wings?

9. Glue your final craft supply selections to the paper.

10. Hang up your wild expressions to share and enjoy!

Let It Snow Snowflakes

Make festive decorations of your favorite wintertime activities to hang up or give away.

TIME TOGETHER: 30 min. PLUS OVERNIGHT TO DRY

GATHER THESE ITEMS:

- 1 sheet or more of drawings, paintings, or other artwork for cutting (plain construction paper will also work)
- 2 pairs of scissors—1 for you and 1 for your grandkiddo
- Stapler
- Glue

LET'S GET STARTED:

1. Fold and cut a sheet of artwork in half to make 2 rectangles. (You and your grandkiddo will each make a snowflake from 1 half.)

2. Fold your rectangle in half, in half again, and then in half one more time. Unfold the paper to see the 8 sections made by the creases.

3. Refold the creases like an accordion to make each fold go back and forth. (Tip: You will have to reverse the direction of some of your first folds.)

4. Fold your paper accordion in half, then unfold.. Staple right in the middle on the crease you just made.

5. Cut your snowflake design on one side with all different shapes—make triangles, squiggles, half-circles, and more. (Tip: Cut out a shape from the end so that the snowflake opens properly.)

6. Fold your paper in half and trace the shapes you cut out on the other side, then unfold. Cut around the traced lines.

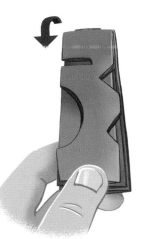

7. Glue one side of the stack, then fold it in half in the other direction. Press together until dry (and leave overnight if needed).

8. Once dry, slowly unfold and unwrap your snowflake until it forms a circle.

9. Add glue to 1 of the 2 remaining ends and press them together. (Tip: This part can be tricky, so use all 4 of your hands together!)

10. Repeat the steps to make a second snowflake together while talking about your favorite winter memories.

11. Hang your snowflakes alone to admire their shapes, or together to create a flurry of memories!

Leaf Animals

Collect items from nature to make your own animal art.

4. Place your books on top of the wax paper.

5. Don't touch! Wait about a week to dry your leaves. If not, close the wax paper again, put the books back on top, and wait another few days.

TIME TOGETHER: 60 min.

PLUS ABOUT A WEEK TO DRY

GATHER THESE ITEMS:

- 15 or more leaves (see step 1)
- Large piece of wax paper
- 3 or more hardcover books
- A few sheets of paper
- 2 pairs of scissors—1 for you and 1 for your grandkiddo
- Glue
- Optional: Grass, seeds, or googly eyes

MAKE THE ANIMALS

1. Remove your dried leaves from the wax paper.

2. Grab a sheet of paper for each of you and play! Talk together about your favorite animals and what they look like.

3. Use scissors to shape the leaves if you need. Make the shapes of an animal's head, legs, and perhaps a tail with your leaves.

4. Glue the leaves to your papers.

5. Use grass, seeds, or googly eyes to add details to your leaf animals.

LET'S GET STARTED:

PRESS THE LEAVES

1. Go on a nature walk together and collect 15 or more leaves of different types, sizes, shapes, and colors.

2. Fold your large piece of wax paper in half, then unfold..

3. Place all the leaves flat on 1 half of the wax paper, then fold the other half over the leaves to close them inside.

6. Display your leafy friends! Share together: What are their names? What are their special features or abilities?

3 Stones in a Row

Play tic-tac-toe and share stories of times you've spent together.

TIME TOGETHER: **45 min.** PLUS A FEW HOURS TO DRY

GATHER THESE ITEMS:

- 10 smooth stones (see step 1)
- Acrylic or tempera paint
- A few small paintbrushes
- Newspaper or other scrap paper
- Clear spray sealer (Grandpas only!)
- String

LET'S GET STARTED:

1. Go on a nature walk together and collect 10 smooth stones.

2. Back inside, wash and dry your stones.

3. Lay down newspaper or scrap paper to cover your work area.

4. Talk together about a favorite day or memory. What reminds you of that day? Choose one image each from the memory and paint it on 5 stones. Let the paint dry for a few hours.

5. **(Grandpas only!)** In a safe location, follow the instructions on the spray sealer to cover each stone, then let the sealer dry.

6. Cut the string into 4 strands about half as long as your grandkiddo's arm.

7. Lay down the strands to form a tic-tac-toe board.

8. Take turns placing one stone at a time in a box. You'll win if you get 3 of the same image in a row.

TO PLAY CHECKERS, PAINT 12 ADDITIONAL STONES EACH AND ADD MORE STRINGS FOR A FULL BOARD!

Mini Spirograph Solar Systems

Spin and trace these geometric designs to create your own imaginary solar systems together.

GATHER THESE ITEMS:

- Masking tape roll
- Large piece of corrugated cardboard
- Scissors
- Hole punch
- Colored pencils
- 1 or more wide rubber bands
- Paper

LET'S GET STARTED:

1. Trace around the inside of your masking tape roll onto your piece of cardboard.

2. Remove the masking tape roll and draw another circle right inside of your first.

3. Cut out the smaller circle of cardboard.

4. Punch out 2 or more holes anywhere on the cardboard circle.

5. Stretch your wide rubber band around the outside edge of your cardboard circle. (Tip: Work together—this tricky job is perfect for 4 hands!)

6. Lay your masking tape roll on top of a piece of paper and drop the cardboard circle inside.

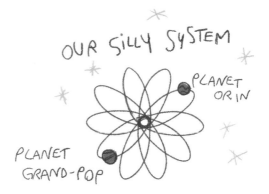

9. Look at your favorite spirograph designs and imagine them as solar systems: What planets are there? Who (or what!) lives on them? How can you travel to reach them? Share your stories together.

MAKE ANOTHER SMALLER CARDBOARD CIRCLE TO SEE HOW THE DESIGNS CHANGE!

7. Hold the masking tape roll steady with one hand. Place a colored pencil into one of the punched holes with the other hand. Slowly use your pencil to roll the cardboard around the inside edge of the masking tape and watch the beautiful patterns appear.

8. Take turns! Create more spirographs by using another color or by placing your pencil in a different hole.

Grandpa and Me Journal

Create a record of your thoughts, dreams, jokes, and time together.

TIME TOGETHER: 60 min.

GATHER THESE ITEMS:

- ☆ Cardstock from page 91
- Large empty cereal box
- Pencil
- 9 sheets of light-colored paper
- Drawing tools like crayons, colored pencils, or markers
- 2 pairs of scissors—1 for you and 1 for your grandkiddo
- Hole punch
- A piece of yarn or string about 4 times as long as your grandkiddo's arm
- Glue
- Optional: Acrylic or tempera paint, paintbrush

LET'S GET STARTED:

1. Open up the seams of your cereal box until it lies flat.

2. Place a sheet of paper in the middle of the flattened box, avoiding the seams, and trace around it with a pencil.

3. Cut out the traced rectangle and fold it in half to make your journal cover.

4. Decorate and draw on your cover together: Use drawing tools on the plain side, or paint on the printed side. (Tip: If you chose paint, let the cover dry before going to the next step.)

5. Punch a hole over the top end of the cover's crease, then repeat on the bottom end of the crease.

6. Line up and fold in half 3 sheets of your paper. Press hard on the thick crease to make a crisp edge. Repeat with the other pages, so that you have 3 folded stacks of 3 pages each.

7. In one stack, punch a hole over 1 end of the crease, then repeat on the other end. Repeat with the other 2 stacks of folded paper.

8. Line up all 3 stacks of paper and start binding your journal: Pull an end of your string through the top-right hole inside the folded papers.

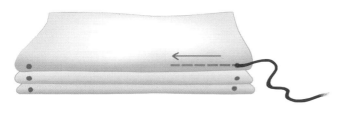

9. Follow the path: Weave inside the stack to the left, down, inside the stack to the right, down, inside the stack and out the bottom left. Pull tight.

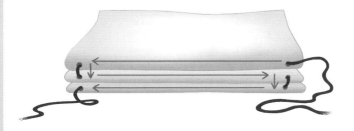

10. Take the loose end of string from the top-right hole and follow the next path: down, inside the stack to the left, down, inside the stack and out the bottom right. Pull tight.

11. Line up your stacks in the cover and pull each loose end of string through the closest hole.

12. From the outside, pull each string up or down the spine and in the other hole. Both strings are now on the inside. Pull them into a tight knot and trim the ends.

13. Cut out the journal prompts from your cardstock sheet. Read the prompts on both sides, choose the ones you like best, and glue them at the tops of the pages. Leave some pages blank for writing your own prompts.

14. Fill in the journal together!

Remember Today Time Capsule

Time flies! Record the details of today so you can reflect anytime you want.

TIME TOGETHER: 60 min.

GATHER THESE ITEMS:

- ☆ Cardstock from page 93
- Drawing tools like crayons, colored pencils, or markers
- 5 sheets of colorful paper
- Large manila envelope
- Ribbon or string
- 2 pairs of scissors—1 for you and 1 for your grandkiddo
- Glue

LET'S GET STARTED:

1. Decorate and draw on your manila envelope.

2. Cut out the time capsule labels and prompts from your cardstock sheet.

3. Ask your grandkiddo to stand up tall. Hold the ribbon up high next to them until it touches the ground, then cut the piece where it marks the height of your grandkiddo.

4. With your grandkiddo's help, cut a second piece of ribbon to mark your own height. (Tip: While you probably won't grow [or shrink] it will be neat to see how much closer your heights get as your grandkiddo grows!)

5. Trace and cut out each of your right hands from the same piece of colorful paper.

6. Glue the hands together with the palms aligned at the bottom, facing the same direction.

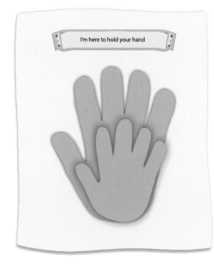

I'm here to hold your hand

7. Fold 2 pieces of colorful paper into quarters, then give 1 paper to yourself and 1 to your grandkiddo.

8. Glue a prompt in each of the 4 boxes. Then use drawing tools to respond to the prompts, sharing aloud as you go.

9. Fold 2 pieces of colorful paper in half, then unfold. Give 1 paper to yourself and 1 to your grandkiddo.

10. Glue labels on the top and bottom boxes. Then use your drawing tools to respond, sharing aloud as you go.

11. When you are done, place all your recordings and responses into the time capsule. (Tip: Add any other crafts from this book that you'd like to save for the future!) Write the date on the seal, then glue it on the close of the envelope.

12. Open and share your time capsule sometime in the future. How long can you wait?

Odd Dot

Odd Dot is a registered trademark of Macmillan Publishing Group, LLC

120 Broadway, New York, New York 10271

OddDot.com

Text copyright © 2023 by Megan Hewes Butler

Illustrations copyright © 2023 by Francesca De Luca

All rights reserved.

COVER DESIGNER Christina Quintero

INTERIOR DESIGNER Kayleigh McCann

EDITOR Kate Avino

ISBN 978-1-250-80414-3

Our books may be purchased in bulk for promotional, educational, or business use. Please contact your local bookseller or the Macmillan Corporate and Premium Sales Department at (800) 221-7945 ext. 5442 or by email at MacmillanSpecialMarkets@macmillan.com.

First edition, 2023

Printed in China by RR Donnelley Asia Printing Solutions Ltd., Dongguan City, Guangdong Province

1 3 5 7 9 10 8 6 4 2

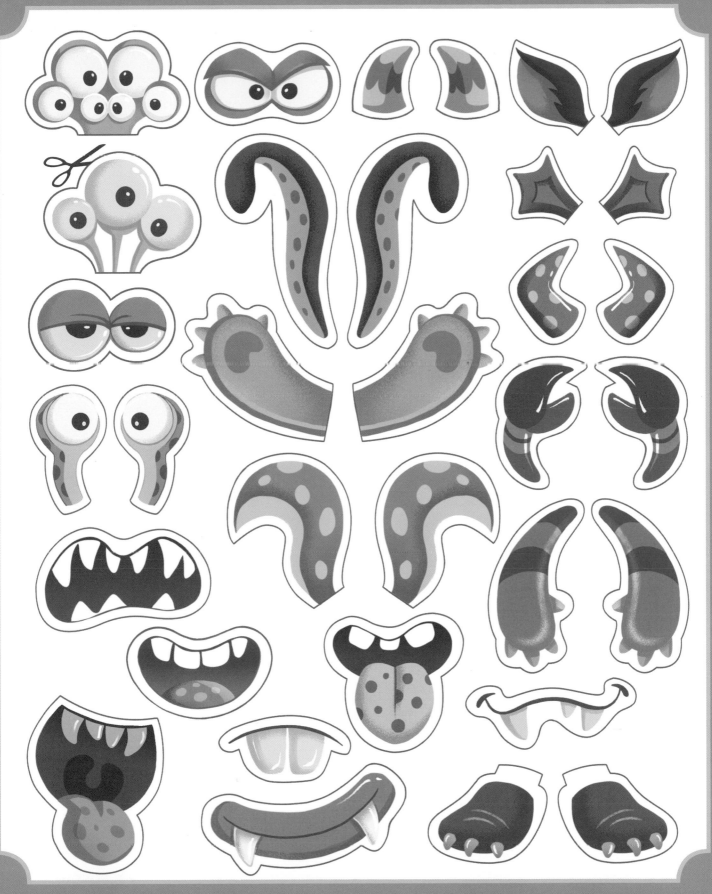

Custom Paper Gliders

Aircraft Target Practice

Any–Day Crackers

You Are My Sunshine Painting

Secret Message Cipher

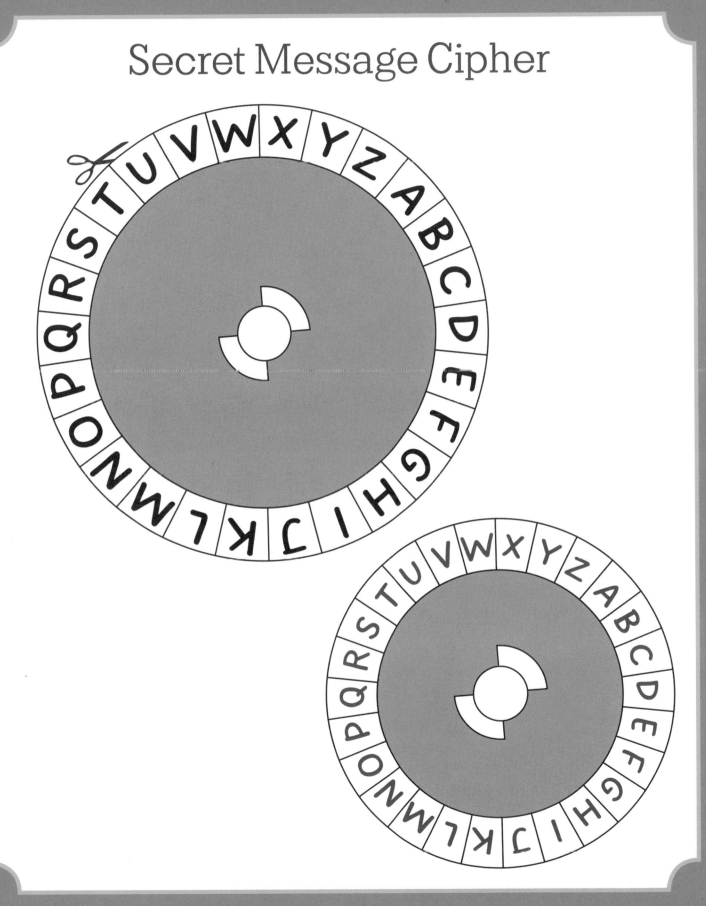

Yarn Art
Cards

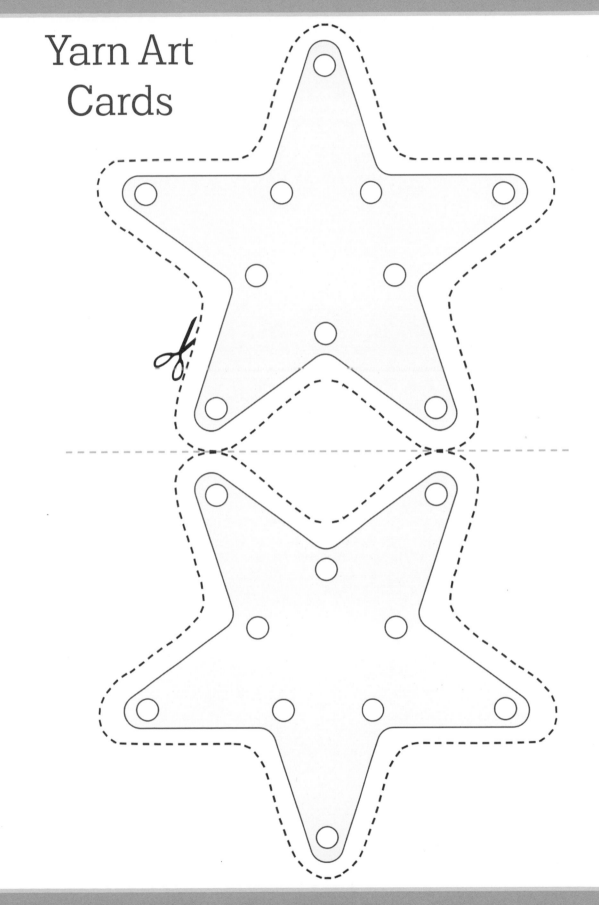

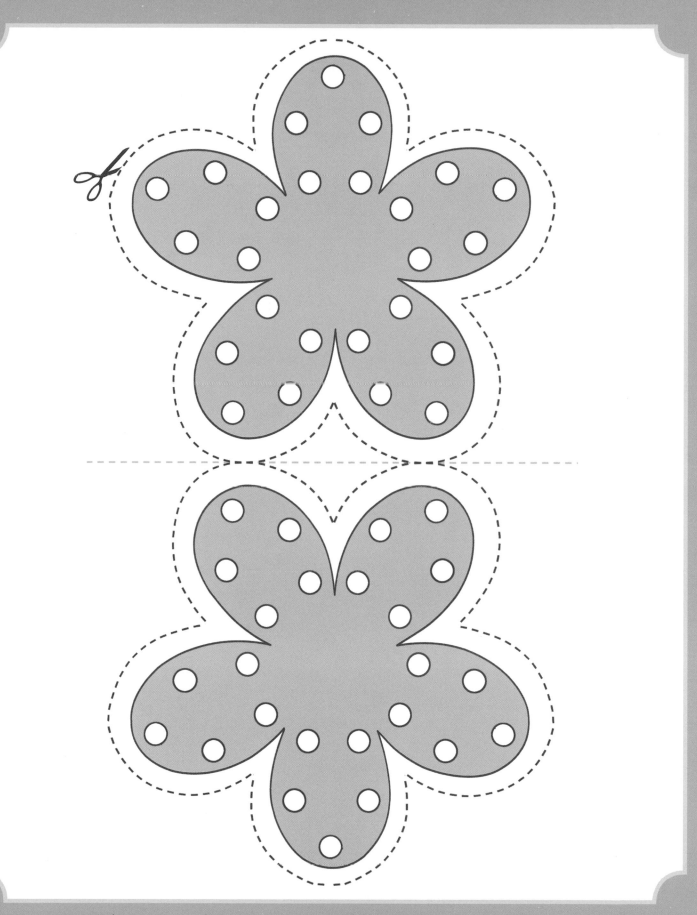

Tower of Memories

Growing in Thankfulness

Warm Fuzzies Bowl

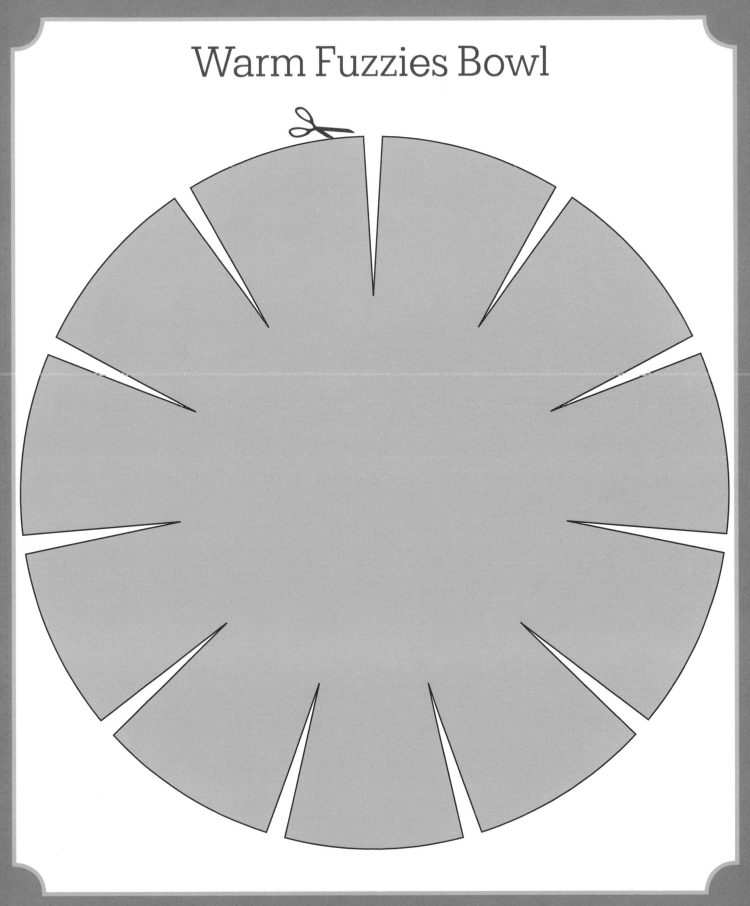

Hanging Together Wall Art

Hanging Together Wall Art: Instructions on page **44**

85

A Bouquet to Share

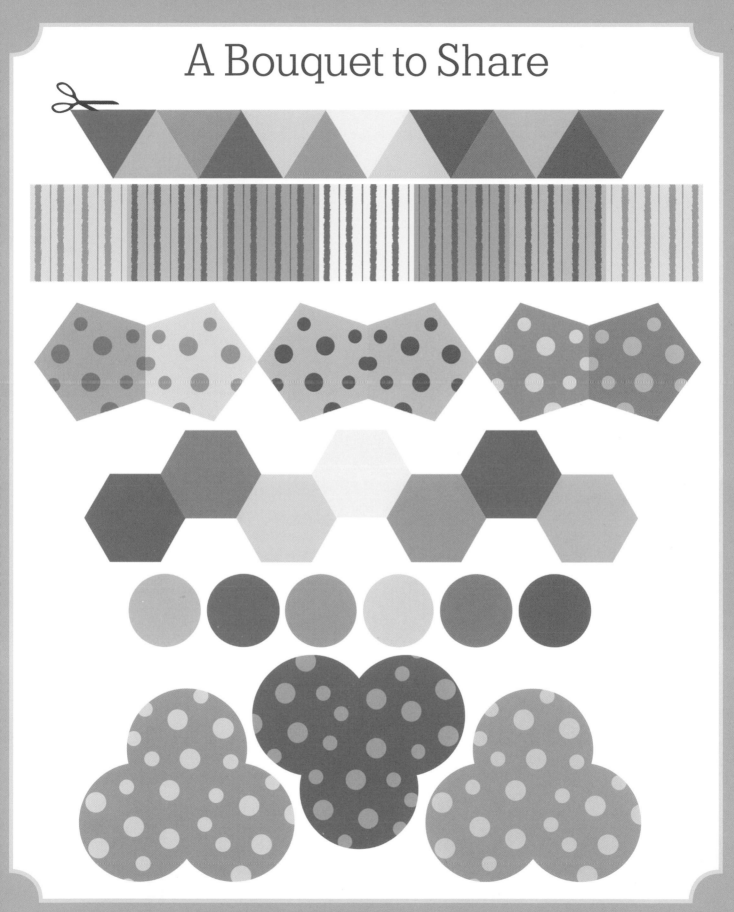

A Bouquet to Share: Instructions on page **46**

Artwork All Year Calendar

JANUARY	FEBRUARY	MARCH	APRIL	MAY	JUNE	JULY	AUGUST	SEPTEMBER	OCTOBER	NOVEMBER	DECEMBER
1	1	1	1	1	1	1	1	1	1	1	1
2	2	2	2	2	2	2	2	2	2	2	2
3	3	3	3	3	3	3	3	3	3	3	3
4	4	4	4	4	4	4	4	4	4	4	4
5	5	5	5	5	5	5	5	5	5	5	5
6	6	6	6	6	6	6	6	6	6	6	6
7	7	7	7	7	7	7	7	7	7	7	7
8	8	8	8	8	8	8	8	8	8	8	8
9	9	9	9	9	9	9	9	9	9	9	9
10	10	10	10	10	10	10	10	10	10	10	10
11	11	11	11	11	11	11	11	11	11	11	11
12	12	12	12	12	12	12	12	12	12	12	12
13	13	13	13	13	13	13	13	13	13	13	13
14	14	14	14	14	14	14	14	14	14	14	14
15	15	15	15	15	15	15	15	15	15	15	15
16	16	16	16	16	16	16	16	16	16	16	16
17	17	17	17	17	17	17	17	17	17	17	17
18	18	18	18	18	18	18	18	18	18	18	18
19	19	19	19	19	19	19	19	19	19	19	19
20	20	20	20	20	20	20	20	20	20	20	20
21	21	21	21	21	21	21	21	21	21	21	21
22	22	22	22	22	22	22	22	22	22	22	22
23	23	23	23	23	23	23	23	23	23	23	23
24	24	24	24	24	24	24	24	24	24	24	24
25	25	25	25	25	25	25	25	25	25	25	25
26	26	26	26	26	26	26	26	26	26	26	26
27	27	27	27	27	27	27	27	27	27	27	27
28	28	28	28	28	28	28	28	28	28	28	28
29	29	29	29	29	29	29	29	29	29	29	29
30		30	30	30	30	30	30	30	30	30	30
31		31		31		31	31		31		31

IF YOU COULD INVENT A NEW FOOD, WHAT WOULD IT LOOK LIKE?
WHAT WOULD IT TASTE LIKE?

DATE:

IF YOU COULD HAVE ONE SECRET WAY TO EXPLORE—FLYING, HOLDING YOUR BREATH
UNDERWATER FOR A DAY, OR BEING INVISIBLE—WHICH WOULD YOU CHOOSE?

DATE:

WHAT TOPPINGS WOULD YOU PUT ON THE ULTIMATE BIRTHDAY CAKE?
WHO WOULD YOU SHARE IT WITH?

DATE:

IF YOU COULD TRAVEL TO ANY PLACE ON EARTH, WHERE WOULD IT BE?

DATE:

WHAT WOULD YOUR DREAM FORT LOOK LIKE?

DATE:

SHARE A MEMORY OF A TIME SOMEONE WAS KIND TO YOU.

DATE:

WHAT WOULD YOUR DREAM CASTLE LOOK LIKE?

DATE:

SHARE A MEMORY OF A TIME YOU WERE KIND TO SOMEONE.

DATE:

IF YOU COULD HAVE ANY ANIMAL FOR A PET, WHAT WOULD IT BE?
WHERE WOULD YOU KEEP IT?

DATE:

IF YOU COULD GROW TO THE SIZE OF A LARGE DINOSAUR FOR A DAY,
WHERE WOULD YOU EXPLORE?

DATE:

WHAT ARE YOUR 3 FAVORITE THINGS THAT ARE THE COLOR GREEN?

DATE:

IF YOU COULD TALK TO ROCKS OR CLOUDS, WHICH WOULD YOU CHOOSE?
WHAT WOULD YOU ASK?

DATE:

WHAT WAS YOUR FAVORITE PART OF LAST WEEKEND?

DATE:

WHAT IS YOUR FAVORITE ANIMAL? WHY IS IT YOUR FAVORITE?

DATE:

IF YOU COULD DESIGN YOUR OWN ICE CREAM CONE—ANY SIZE, SHAPE, AND
DESIGN—WHAT WOULD IT LOOK LIKE?

DATE:

WHAT WOULD YOUR DREAM SUBMARINE LOOK LIKE?

DATE:

IF YOU COULD BE SOMEONE ELSE FOR A DAY, WHO WOULD YOU BE?
WHAT WOULD YOU DO?

DATE:

IF YOU COULD HAVE 3 SUPERPOWERS, WHAT WOULD THEY BE?

DATE:

WHAT ARE YOUR 3 FAVORITE THINGS THAT ARE THE COLOR ORANGE?

DATE:

IF YOU COULD MAGICALLY BECOME THE WORLD'S BEST AT ANY SKILL,
WHAT WOULD IT BE?

DATE:

IF YOU COULD CHANGE THE SOUND THAT RAIN MAKES, WHAT WOULD IT SOUND LIKE?
HOW WOULD YOUR FAMILY REACT TO THE NEW SOUND?

DATE:

IF YOU COULD DESIGN YOUR OWN WATER SLIDE, WHAT WOULD IT LOOK LIKE?
WHAT WOULD IT BE MADE OF?

DATE:

WHAT DO YOU THINK IS THE BEST JOB IN THE WHOLE WORLD?

DATE:

IF YOU COULD CHANGE ONE SCHOOL RULE, WHAT WOULD IT BE?

DATE:

IMAGINE THAT YOU JUMPED OVER A MAGICAL PUDDLE AND KEPT GOING UP, UP, UP.
WHERE WOULD YOU GO?

DATE:

IF YOU WERE GOING ON A TRIP TO THE ARCTIC, WHAT WOULD YOU PACK?

DATE:

IF YOU COULD YELL ONE THING SO LOUDLY THAT YOUR ENTIRE STATE COULD HEAR
YOU, WHAT WOULD IT BE?

DATE:

WHAT IS ONE THING YOU ARE THANKFUL FOR TODAY?

DATE:

IF YOU COULD HAVE A PET WORM OR PET LLAMA, WHICH WOULD YOU CHOOSE?

DATE:

IF YOU COULD SPEND A DAY RIDING A WHALE OR BEING IN OUTER SPACE,
WHICH WOULD YOU CHOOSE?

DATE:

IF YOU COULD DESIGN A NEW PLAYGROUND—ANY SIZE, SHAPE, COLOR, AND
FEATURES—WHAT WOULD IT BE LIKE?

DATE:

WHAT IS YOUR FAVORITE HOLIDAY? WHAT DO YOU LIKE TO DO TO CELEBRATE?

DATE:

Remember Today Time Capsule

I'M HERE TO HOLD YOUR HAND!

IF YOU COULD DO ANYTHING WITH YOUR GRANDKIDDO TODAY, WHAT WOULD IT BE?

IF YOU COULD DO ANYTHING WITH YOUR GRANDPA TODAY, WHAT WOULD IT BE?

WHAT IS ONE THING YOU LOVE MOST ABOUT YOUR GRANDKIDDO?

WHAT IS ONE THING YOU LOVE MOST ABOUT YOUR GRANDPA?

WHEN DID YOU LAUGH THE MOST TOGETHER?

WHEN DID YOU LAUGH THE MOST TOGETHER?

WHAT IS YOUR FAVORITE PLACE TO GO TOGETHER?

WHAT IS YOUR FAVORITE PLACE TO GO TOGETHER?